The

Charles Sherlock is engaged in training ministers, as a lecturer at Ridley College, Melbourne.
Peta Sherlock is chaplain of a girls' secondary school, Lowther Hall, Melbourne.

The God book

Much more than a role-play game

Charles and Peta Sherlock

frameworks

FRAMEWORKS
38 De Montfort Street, Leicester LE1 7GP, England

© Charles and Peta Sherlock, 1990

Unless otherwise stated, Scripture quotations in this publication are from the Holy Bible, New International Version. Copyright © 1973, 1978, 1984 International Bible Society. Published in Great Britain by Hodder and Stoughton Ltd.

First published 1990

British Library Cataloguing in Publication Data
Sherlock, Charles, *1945–*
    The God book: much more than a role-play game.
    1. Christianity
    I. Title   II. Sherlock, Peta, *1946–*
200

ISBN 0–85111–130–0

Set in 10 on 11½ Palatino
Phototypeset in Great Britain by
Input Typesetting Ltd, London SW19 8DR
Printed in Great Britain by
Cox & Wyman Ltd, Reading

Frameworks is an imprint of Inter-Varsity Press, the book-publishing division of the Universities and Colleges Christian Fellowship.

In memory of David Penman,
an OK minister who liked football.

This book is about God.

And about helping you sort out your ideas about life.

If you want to get your ideas straight, it will probably mean cleaning out some old rubbish. You may be attached to this rubbish. The head-cleaning might hurt a bit. But a wise man once said, 'You can't think decently if you don't want to hurt yourself.'

To be honest, we'd like to introduce you to the God that Christians believe in. But there's no obvious or right way through these pages and you are allowed to enjoy the book!

The main character in the story is the person you see in the mirror. You.

To make a good story better, we've given you a family and a job. A brother Pete, who has a girlfriend Kate. Your Dad, Charlie, is a no-nonsense type. Mum likes making sure you look after yourself in the flat you rent. Randolph is the sort of cousin you'd rather not have. (Sorry to all the Randolphs out there!) Especially important is Aunt Jane. Reg was an old friend of hers.

Your new family is designed to help you get your ideas sorted out. But if this sort of masochism is not for you, then:

1 *Put this book back on the shelf now.* ***OR***
2 *Give it to your friend for Christmas (because they gave you a rotten, framed photo of Kylie Minogue last year).* ***OR***
3 *Turn the page and begin the adventure because you haven't the faintest idea what masochism is anyway.*

If you do choose 3 (and we hope you do) you may find yourself going round in circles. Don't get flustered. After all, that's what life is like sometimes!

If you get fed up, you can always open the book and pick a page at random. Or try page 77. Or begin again. We think all the pages are worth reading anyway!

(***Please turn to page 2.***)

You've always had a soft spot for your Aunt Jane. Not that you spent a lot of time with her. It's just that, in the way of some maiden aunts, she always treated you like a human being. She drew out your hopes and plans for the future. But she never asked dumb questions when you were young like, 'What do you want to be when you grow up?'

She could show you round her garden without being boring. She even wall-papered the loo with magazine pictures. It was fun to visit to see what the toilet scenery was this month.

She was also very good at getting the family together for Christmas and other holidays. But it always seemed strange to you that other members of the family tended to laugh at her behind her back.

Funny that you should be so attached to her, and yet be one of the last to know she had cancer. Of course, Aunt Jane would never mention the subject. She just continued on, putting up with the pain, until this week. She died quietly in her sleep the night before last. She was only 56, not a bad innings I suppose.

The funeral is early next week, at the local church where Jane was a regular. Funerals are not the most pleasant things are they?

You think about whether you should go:

1 'I think I'd like to go to the funeral.' (**turn to page 17**)
2 'I'll phone Pete, to see if he's going.' (Remember Pete? He's your brother.) (**turn to page 4**)
3 'Can't make up my mind yet.' (**turn to page 5**)
4 'I don't really want to go, but I will send flowers.' (**turn to page 8**)

'Love makes the world go round.' Or so the song says. And you agree. Aunt Jane would have, too, you think – but would have brought God into it, somehow. 'God is love,' she'd say, though you weren't sure exactly what she meant.

And you *did* love Aunt Jane. She could be annoying. She had funny ideas about some things. But she never let her ideas get in the way of her friendships. Even with Kate.

You think you may be looking forward to the funeral now. 'A good chance to pay my respects, to show I did love my aunt.' But you're also a bit worried. 'Funerals aren't exactly my idea of fun.'

The family will be there in force. Some of them don't get on very well. A few are definitely anti-religious, too. They'll go out of respect for Aunt Jane, and to say their goodbyes. But it'll be a tense time for everyone.

How do you feel about going?

1 *'Funerals are only to show respect to the dead, and say your goodbyes. God has nothing to do with it.'* (**turn to page 36**)
2 *'The funeral will be a good way to say goodbye, and also to say thank you to God for Aunt Jane.'* (**turn to page 23**)
3 *'I'm not sure. I'd like to think about it a bit longer.'* (**turn to page 5**)
4 *'I'll ring Pete and see what he's doing.'* (**turn to page 11**)

Can't make up your own mind? You'll ring your brother, Pete. Though you don't normally ask his opinion about anything. In fact, you've never really seen eye to eye with him since he went off with Kate at that party six months ago.

'But this is different. It's a family matter now. He might be glad of the chance to talk,' you think. 'After all, we both had some great holidays with Aunt Jane when we were kids.'

Remember her lovely big garden with a huge tree at the bottom? She let you take out blankets and cushions, and you and Pete even slept out one night up there. Peanut butter sandwiches have never tasted so good. Not that you slept well. It was so dark and there were lots of noises, but it was fun. You never did that at home.

She had a big box with her treasures from all over the world. Old books, and maps, and pictures of churches, an old cross, and bundles of brown postcards and lots more. Even some really old bits of stone and metal that she said came from hundreds of years ago.

What would you like to do now?

1 *'It's nice to think about the good old days with Aunt Jane.'* (**turn to page 12**)
2 *'I'm going to ring Pete now.'* (**turn to page 11**)

'Can Aunt Jane really be dead?'

You remember the last time you saw her. She looked so pale and weak, but her eyes were full of life. She was quiet for most of your visit, but asked you to be sure to keep an eye on her cat.

Perhaps she knew she hadn't long left. Did she want you to have something to remember her by? Or to have something to keep you occupied?

You still feel quite upset by the news. Even though it wasn't a surprise, it's given you a shake. It's not the sort of thing that happens every day.

What will you do next?

1 *Ring your brother Pete to have a talk.* (**turn to page 11**)
2 *Go round to see how your aunt's cat is.* (**turn to page 13**)
3 *Have a quiet evening to think about it further.* (**turn to page 20**)

You're right, of course. No-one could be that good. Aunt Jane wasn't perfect. You only have to think of how other family members nodded and winked behind her back.

'Wasn't there some story, way back in her past. A man? Aunt Jane and men! Hard to imagine.' You remember some of those old photos of her as a young woman with Mum. 'Awful clothes, but not bad looking.'

You wonder if Pete knows any more about that business with the man. It seems a bit rude to want to talk about it, though. You're supposed to be thinking about her funeral. Not the secrets in her closet.

Aunt Jane would have said 'I'm not perfect, just forgiven.' That was her favourite line. 'Not perfect, just forgiven. I can cope with others because God has coped with me,' she'd say.

It occurs to you that your aunt was actually quite a religious person. Funny that it hadn't occurred to you before this. Seems obvious, really.

Would you like to:

1 *Ring Pete and ask if he's going to the funeral? (You might be able to ask casually about that man from her past.)* (**turn to page 11**)
2 *Think some more about your aunt and what made her tick?* (**turn to page 14**)
3 *Look at what Christians think about sex. You can't imagine Aunt Jane and a man. Christians and sex don't mix in your experience.* (**turn to page 71**)

You feel pleased with yourself knowing that your presence at the funeral will be constructive. In fact, if saying prayers and things might help Aunt Jane get to heaven, why shouldn't it help you too?

'Why don't you listen to me?' screams the religious nut looking right at you. 'No-one is good enough to get to heaven!'

'But surely being religious helps,' you think.

'Being religious doesn't help!' he cries.

'Not even praying?' you wonder.

'Not even praying helps!' he yells.

You begin to feel a bit intimidated because the nut seems to read your thoughts.

'You may feel intimidated, as if I can read your thoughts, but I tell you only Jesus can help you get into heaven!'

'So that's it,' you think. 'Getting into heaven is not to do with being religious. It's to do with Jesus.'

Beating a hasty retreat before this man reads any more of your mind, you:

1 *Resolve to find out more about Jesus.* (**turn to page 39**)
2 *Decide that religion is just for those with mental defects.* (**turn to page 25**)
3 *Turn your back and walk off. You just want to go to the funeral to say goodbye to your aunt.* (**turn to page 36**)
4 *Grab one of his leaflets, smile sweetly and run like hell. Sorry, Freudian slip there.* (**turn to page 57**)

As soon as you walk into the florist's shop you realize that sending a wreath is not an easy option. Especially when a blue-rinse perm and a pair of half-moon glasses appear above a bucket of yellow gladioli. 'Be with you in half a minute, dear.'

Then you see the display of small cards on the counter. It dawns on you that you'll have to send a message with the wreath.

'What will I write?' you wonder. 'Who am I writing to? Who will read it? Aunt Jane? Mum for sure.'

Why *are* you sending the wreath for that matter? So that your mother won't think you're mean and selfish? So that the family will think you did the right thing?

What would you *really* like to do?

1 Write 'With deepest sympathy.' (**turn to page 28**)
2 Write 'With gratitude to a lady who has enriched my life.' (**turn to page 12**)
3 Write 'Dear Aunt Jane, I am so sorry you're dead. The way you lived showed me that death and beyond didn't frighten you.' (You'd like to add 'I'm even afraid of living', but it looks funny on a card and you're running out of space anyway.) (**turn to page 14**)
4 Forget the flowers. 'I'd like to do something positive. I'll send some money to Cancer Research instead of spending it on a wreath.' (**turn to page 59**)
5 You didn't realize a bunch of flowers cost so much. 'Why should I spend my hard-earned cash on something that will be dead in forty-eight hours? I've got better things to do with my money.' (**turn to page 66**)

'Pie in the sky when you die.' That's what some Christians seem to believe. A guy called Karl Marx said the same thing. 'Religion is the opiate of the people.' Sort of like a drug to stop them wanting to change the world.

Some Christians *have* used heaven as the excuse to do nothing to help people.

Jesus would have none of this attitude. He certainly did teach that there's more to life than the here and now. Yet he also got his hands dirty, mixing with real people, and their real problems: the poor, the despised, the sick, the mad, the bad and even the prostitutes.

Jesus taught great truths by which to live. He had a lot to say about what was wrong with the system. But he worked mainly by caring for individuals. He offered hope for the future and showed what it could be like by the way he lived. He even died for them.

There have been lots of Christians who have helped make life more just and peaceful. Like Martin Luther King, who helped black Americans recover their dignity. And Mother Teresa. She's really done a lot.

Religion *can* be misused. But believing in Jesus gives something to live for now, and for ever.

What do you think?

1   *'I'd like to know more about this Jesus.'* (**turn to page 39**)
2   *'Come off it. This book is just another attempt to calm down people who ought to be angry.'* (*Even if this book isn't doing much good, don't let it dirty the environment when you get rid of it. Put it in the bin – please.*)
3   *'Christianity isn't for me. I just want to go to my aunt's funeral and get it over with.'* (**turn to page 60**)
4   *'Now if Christianity had something to say about the state of the economy, that would be different! Money is what really matters.'* (**turn to page 66**)

PS You can find Jesus' teaching in the Bible. The section by Matthew, chapters 5 to 7, gives a good sample.

The more you think about Dad, the more you feel you just don't know him. You know about him, of course. His gardening, his job, his bowls, and, a few years ago, his heart turn. But you don't know him.

Not like you knew Aunt Jane. She understood you, even when she disapproved. You felt accepted by her. Dad was always distant.

As a child you went to ask him questions, and his answers satisfied you. But, just recently, you've begun to wonder.

One time you asked him why he never went to church like Aunt Jane did.

'I've no time for that religion nonsense,' he replied. 'Religion is just for the weak. Emotional cripples who need crutches. God helps those who help themselves. That's what I say. Work hard and keep yourself busy. That's what life's about.'

What do you think?

1 *'I need something to do. I'll feed Aunt Jane's cat.'* (**turn to page 13**)
2 *'I think Dad was right. Life is all about being busy and working hard.'* (**turn to page 46**)
3 *'I agree with Dad. Religion is for the weak.'* (**turn to page 25**)

You dial Pete's place.

'Hi, Pete. Long time no see. How's life? Have you heard about Aunt Jane? Sad, isn't it. I still can't believe she's not here anymore.'

'Yes. A nasty business. When's the funeral?'

'Next week. Are you going?' you ask.

'Don't know. I hate funerals,' replies Pete.

'Mum will expect us to turn up.'

'Since when do you do everything your parents tell you?'

'Well, I'd really like to go, in a way,' you respond. 'But I'd also like to think of her as she was. Not in some wooden box in the ground.'

'Where is the funeral? At her church?' he asks. 'I can't stand that minister. He's such a bore,' he goes on. 'Don't ask me why she ever went to that place.'

'Pete, I hate talking over the phone,' you admit. 'Would you like to meet for a drink at the pub?'

'I'm happy just to meet up at the funeral,' he replies. 'But if you really want to talk, I'm going to the pub anyway tonight.'

He hangs up. 'Drat! I forgot to ask him about the man in Aunt Jane's past.' Maybe just as well you didn't. 'Let sleeping dogs lie,' you think.

Which do you decide to do?

1 Meet up at the funeral? (**turn to page 60**)
2 Meet in the pub with Pete? (**turn to page 38**)

Aunt Jane certainly enriched your life.

When you were in tennis competitions she sometimes came and watched you play. Always had something encouraging to say, something good to say about you. Even if you hadn't played well.

You could tell her your plans, your hopes, and know that she wouldn't laugh. When you told her you planned to play tennis professionally, she was interested to hear all about it. Most people took no notice. Aunt Jane was such a good listener.

She also told great stories when you were a kid. That old treasure box of hers must have had a thousand in it. All of them got back eventually to the story of Jesus.

Only a few months ago you visited her. You knew then that she must have been very ill. Yet she seemed to be so interested in your latest plans and hopes.

What do you think?

1 *'I'm sick of this Aunt Jane. No-one could be that good.'* (**turn to page 6**)
2 *'She was so positive about people and being alive. What did she have that made her different?'* (**turn to page 14**)

Cats aren't your favourite animal. But they're OK. 'They can be good company,' you think. 'They remember who you are if you feed them.'

You have to go down the side path of Aunt Jane's house to get to her back garden. It seems so empty with her gone. You find the cat's bowls are empty. You fill the water bowl and find a packet of cat food in the shed. 'Here puss! Here puss!'

A rather straggly tabby pops its head from behind the shed, warily moves to the food, and begins to eat hungrily. Another cat appears over the side fence. It is jet-black, well-cared for. Its sharp yellow eyes stare at you. It walks right across your path, and hisses at the tabby.

You're puzzled. 'Did Aunt Jane own two cats? Surely hers wouldn't be black?'

You react by:

1 *Chasing the tabby away. It's obviously a stray. (**turn to page 16**)*
2 *Shivering. 'Black cats give me the creeps.' (**turn to page 27**)*

It suddenly becomes clear to you.

Aunt Jane was a card-carrying Christian! She went to church regularly. She had that treasure box full of religious junk. At least three Bibles. She talked about Jesus and forgiveness and God and love and so on. And, in the end, she wasn't afraid of death.

And yet she wasn't exactly religious. She wasn't a Bible-basher. She was simply a very good human-being who loved Jesus and God.

Funny. You've always thought of Christians as boring, stupid fuddy-duddies. That's not quite Aunt Jane, though. Well, maybe she was a bit stupid. People seemed to take advantage of her. But she never seemed to mind.

'Oh God! Does this mean that she had her act together because she was a Christian?'

What do you reckon?

1 *'Some people need religion more than others. It's all to do with your personality.'* (**turn to page 25**)

2 *'All the Christians I've met are boring old fuddy-duddies who pray all the time. Aunt Jane was an exception.'* (**turn to page 81**)

3 *'If this Christian God really exists, why did he let Aunt Jane die of cancer?'* (**turn to page 30**)

4 *'Why do Christians always go on about sin?'* (**turn to page 64**)

5 *'Oh no! I've just said "Oh God!". Will I be struck down for blasphemy?'* (**turn to page 68**)

You *do* know Aunt Jane was a really great person. What you don't know is whether you believe in God and heaven. But it would be nice to send some flowers to say goodbye.

On your way to the florist to buy some black flowers (which seemed a good compromise at the time) you notice one of those religious nuts preaching in the shopping centre.

'Being a good person is not enough!' he screams. 'No-one is good enough to get to heaven. Not one of you is going there!' He looks right at you.

What do you feel?

1 *'What does he know, silly old fool? No loving God would send Aunt Jane anywhere but heaven!'* (**turn to page 19**)
2 *'I really* **must** *go to the funeral. My prayers might make all the difference.'* (**turn to page 7**)
3 *'I wonder if Aunt Jane knew that? I'd better have a word with this character and see what I can do.'* (**turn to page 21**)
4 *'Forget it. I'm not going to let him spoil my day. I just want to go to the funeral to show my love and respect for my aunt.'* (**turn to page 3**)

Did that make you feel better? Now Aunt Jane's cat can have a good feed.

'What did she call her?' You can't remember. 'I'll pick a name myself. How about "Blackie"?' you think. 'No. She would never have chosen such a boring name.'

But would your aunt have sent a hungry tabby away like that? She used to feed the odd stray, and keep an eye on them. At one stage she'd collected three or four. Gave each one a name from the Bible. Matthew, Malachi, Michael, Mordecai. . .

Yet she'd take them to the cat's home if she couldn't look after them. 'Love means you have to be realistic,' she'd say. 'Feeding hungry people is more important than collecting stray cats.'

Quite a thinker, Aunt Jane!

Do you want to:

1 *Think more about Aunt Jane's beliefs?* (**turn to page 14**)
2 *Get on with looking after her cat?* (**turn to page 29**)
3 *Return home and ring Pete?* (**turn to page 11**)

PS Before you leave this page, have a go at picking a decent name for the cat.

You do want to go to your aunt's funeral. Yet you have a few problems. 'Should I wear black? Do you tip the minister?' for example. 'Which side of the aisle do I sit on?' Even so, now you've made up your mind you feel better.

When you tell your neighbour Mrs Gigglewick that you're going, she looks surprised. 'What on earth do you want to do that for?' she exclaims. 'Life is for the living. You can't do anything for her now!'

Well, what on earth *do* you want to go for?

1 *'I'd like to give my aunt a good send-off.'* (**turn to page 15**)
2 *'I really should have visited her more after she got sick. Perhaps going along will make me feel better.'* (**turn to page 26**)
3 *'I want to show my love for her.'* (**turn to page 3**)
4 *'The family will expect me to be there, and Aunt Jane always was keen on the family.'* (**turn to page 18**)

That *is* funny. Aunt Jane was keen on 'the family'. Yet somehow, now that she's gone it's as if the family has gone, too. Since he fell in with Kate, you've hardly spoken to Pete. You've only seen them at Aunt Jane's get-togethers.

The whole family disapproves of Kate. But, come to think of it, Aunt Jane was the only one who really made any effort to get to know her.

And what about Dad? It doesn't seem as if you know him at all. When you saw him last month he was just the same. Keeping himself busy around the house and the garden. But you never really talked with him.

What do you do?

1   *For Aunt Jane's sake you decide to contact your brother Pete.* (**turn to page 11**)

2   *You start to think more about Dad.* (**turn to page 10**)

3   *Say to yourself, 'What a bunch of hypocrites the family is!'* (**turn to page 33**)

4   *Wonder whether the family will get together at Christmas this year, with Aunt Jane gone.* (**turn to page 49**)

'Wouldn't a loving God send Aunt Jane straight to heaven?' you think. 'Surely she deserves it if anyone does.'

But she did say 'I'm not perfect.' And you don't know everything about her. Why did the rest of the family sneer at her?

'Was my aunt just a hypocrite too?' you wonder. 'Like all the rest of the family?'

You start to ponder:

1 *'Maybe Aunt Jane was a hypocrite. We're all hypocrites. What's the point of it all?'* (**turn to page 33**)
2 *'We all get what we deserve. Anyway, I'd rather go to hell. Like Randolph says, "All my friends will be there!"'* (**turn to page 22**)
3 *'There's no way of knowing anything about heaven or hell or God or any of it until we're dead. And then it's too late anyway.'* (**turn to page 51**)
4 *'Christians don't really believe that God will judge us when we die, do they?'* (**turn to page 55**)

PAGE 20 THE GOD BOOK

'Will I go to the funeral?' you ask yourself. 'I've only been to one funeral before, when I was just a kid.'

You start getting bothered. 'What will I wear? Will I know when to stand up and sit down? From what I've heard, funerals are drab and dreary affairs.'

But, it *is* Aunt Jane's funeral. You *were* fond of her. Perhaps it might be a good way of saying good-bye to her, even if she can't hear you.

Also, that friend of the family might be there, the one you've taken a fancy to! The day off work would be a break. Your boss is making heavy demands on you, and you do feel under pressure.

It will be a Christian funeral, though. You're not sure you believe any of that stuff.

After a lot of to-ing and fro-ing you finally decide:

1 *To go to the funeral.* (**turn to page 60**)
2 *To ring up your brother and do what he does.* (**turn to page 11**)
3 *You don't want to go to the funeral. You'll send flowers instead.* (**turn to page 8**)
4 *To put off the decision a bit longer.* (**turn to page 34**)

'Repent, you sinners!' he shouts right in your face as you try to walk up to him inconspicuously.

'Excuse me . . .' you begin.

'Yes?' He looks as embarrassed as you feel. Probably he is more used to people avoiding him.

'Can I just ask you about heaven and . . .'

He slips quickly back into gear. 'If you were to die tonight and stand before God's judgment seat, what would you say?'

'That's just it,' you blurt out desperately, 'my aunt *has* died. What can I do?'

'Repent and believe . . .'

'No, what can I do about my aunt?'

'She's in God's hands now,' he replies, looking up at the sky. Then he stares right at you. 'I'm asking *you* to answer the question. What if you died tonight . . .'

He gets his big, black Bible out from under his arm. His pockets are bulging with leaflets. You feel as if everyone is staring at you.

Do you:

1 *Walk away as quickly as you can, thinking 'Silly old fool, what does he know? No loving God would send Aunt Jane anywhere but heaven.'* (**turn to page 19**)

2 *Take a leaflet and run.* (**turn to page 57**)

3 *Run, resolving to phone Aunt Jane's minister. He might be a bit more reasonable.* (**turn to page 35**)

Can anyone possibly know what happens after death? Books can't tell you. There's all that business about people who die in the operating theatre and see a light at the end of a tunnel. Then they write a book or go on TV and make a million. But can you prove any of it?

Death is such a lonely business. The one thing we have in common with everybody else. But the one thing no-one else can do for you. You've got to do your own dying.

Your brother's girlfriend Kate reckons she can talk to the dead. Gets out her ouija board and off she goes.

What about heaven and hell? Randolph used to say in his smart way, 'I don't mind going to hell. All my friends will be there.'

'If Randolph is going to be there,' you think to yourself, 'it *will* be hell.'

What do you think?

1   *'I'd like to know more about Christian ideas on death and hell.'* (**turn to page 55**)

2   *'Is there any truth in Kate's ideas?'* (**turn to page 43**)

3   *'Hasn't science disproved all this religion and supernatural business?'* (**turn to page 56**)

(turn to page 55)
(turn to page 43)
(turn to page 56)

Goodbyes can be great. Like the time you went on your overseas holiday. Or terrible, like when Pete and Kate cleared out after a fight.

You feel really torn up about your aunt's death. 'But I know she's in God's hands,' you think. Your love for her is all part of your love for God.

You remember the time old Reg died. Aunt Jane shed a few tears at the funeral, but still sang up loudly. 'I'll miss Reg a lot, but he's safe now. Over his long suffering, at peace,' she told you. 'He trusted Jesus to help him in this life. Now he is with Jesus.'

So you are looking forward to the funeral. 'A good, truly Christian one is terrific,' you reflect. 'It should make you want to cry and shout and laugh and weep all at once. Jesus *did* rise from death, and so will Jane.'

Yet that doesn't make her death – or the death of Jesus, for that matter – any easier, does it? She won't be with you until Jesus comes back. At least, not in a human way. 'But she'll be singing all the songs along with me now, especially in church,' you realize. 'Just a lot better, and in tune!'

Still, the funeral isn't easy to face. You want to:

1　*Ring the minister for a chat.* (**turn to page 35**)

2　*Think about how Jesus can help you.* (**turn to page 69**)

'The minister ought to have some answers. After all, that's what they're paid for, isn't it?'

Mind you, how could you talk to a minister? They seem to live in a different world. When you see them on TV they have funny accents and wear odd clothes. If they are talking about things that really matter, how come they make it seem so dull and uninteresting? 'And what if he gets me to say a prayer?' You're worried.

You spend some time thinking this over. In the end you decide:

1 *'It really would be too hard to go to the funeral. I could never fit in with a church and what goes on there. I'll send flowers instead.'* (**turn to page 8**)
2 *'I really want to get to grips with these questions. It can't do any harm to speak to the minister. I'll phone him.'* (**turn to page 35**)

'Some people need religion more than others,' you think. Your friend, Sandy, had a brain tumour diagnosed two years ago. Coped all right. Had the operation, and is OK now. Never thought about God.

Someone else might have a crisis like that and become really religious. It all depends on your personality. Or how you were brought up.

Randolph, who's been to university, says 'Don't feel guilty about things like sex. They're about mistakes your parents made when you were a baby. Study Freud.'

Freud explained everything with psychology. He said you get your idea of God from what your father was like. 'If God is like my Dad he must be pretty busy, and have no time to talk to me much,' you think.

But Freud based his ideas on problem people, like women who had terrible dark secrets to hide. 'Could that explain Aunt Jane's religion? A terrible dark secret?' But she didn't seem in need of a psychiatrist!

Guilt. Sin. God. Who needs them? Only emotionally weak people. Dad and Randolph agree on that at least.

Yet your aunt is still a problem. She wasn't just an old lady who went to church because she'd nothing better to do with her guilt complexes. She seemed quite well-adjusted. If anyone is a psychological mess . . .

'This psychology business is stupid! Gets you going round in circles!'

1 *Why don't you stop all this head stuff now? Aunt Jane would want you to get on with your life.* (**turn to page 42**)
2 *Well, actually you wish you were more like her. She did have her act together. But you know what she'd say. 'Don't copy me. Jesus is the one to follow!'* (**turn to page 69**)
3 *What if God really is there? Maybe we do imagine him like our fathers, but he might be real all the same. 'Hey, God, are you there?'* (**turn to page 40**)
4 *'I still think religious people have the worst record on sex anyway.'* (**turn to page 71**)

'How could Aunt Jane have had cancer all that time and I never knew?' You feel so bad about it! That nosey Mrs Gigglewick is right, for once. It makes you think.

'What will happen to me?'

You resolve to:

1 *Find out what happens when you die.* (**turn to page 22**)

2 *Buy a couple of six-packs of lager. 'It'll help me forget, and time is a great healer isn't it?'* (**turn to page 37**)

3 *Try to talk to the minister about things.* (**turn to page 24**)

4 *Forget it. 'Religion is just a superstition that some people need. Feeling a little guilt is quite natural.'* (**turn to page 25**)

The last time a black cat walked across your path was the day you broke your arm! 'Fate has played me a dirty trick', you think. 'Sent me here, trying to do the right thing, and then I find Aunt Jane's latest cat is black.'

You remember the time you were camping in her garden, when her house was being fixed. A long ladder ran up the side of the house. The only way up the path was under the ladder. You were scared. Didn't walking under a ladder bring bad luck?

Aunt Jane laughed and laughed. 'You don't believe all that rubbish do you? I didn't think you were so gullible! You can only be hurt by such silly ideas if you let them hurt you.'

And then she ran under the ladder, back and forth about ten times. Nothing happened.

Do you :

1 *Forget your superstitions and ring Pete?* (**turn to page 11**)
2 *Feel even more jittery. After all, she* did *die.* (**turn to page 43**)

'With deepest sympathy.' Well, there's a card with that already printed on. Saves you having to make any decisions. Surely no-one could be offended by that?

'What will the family think?' Mum will be glad you sent something even if you didn't go. Of course, Randolph, your arty cousin, will sneer at a mass-produced card. No-one likes him anyway. 'But will the wreath remind them that I'm not there?'

Then the blue-rinse assistant is there fixing you with her 'deepest sympathy' smile. 'Was it someone very close, dear?' she asks.

You:

1   *Leap at the chance to escape by saying 'No, no, just a relative', pay the money and run.* (**turn to page 58**)

2   *Realize that you are running away from what you really feel. 'I ought to go to the funeral.'* (**turn to page 17**)

3   *Mumble something, pay for a bunch of gladioli and dash out of the shop. 'Why can't I ever make a decision and stick to it?'* (**turn to page 34**)

4   *Rush out and throw up in the gutter. 'People are such hypocrites. Especially in my family.'* (**turn to page 33**)

(Have you named the cat yet? Fill in the blanks please.)
_____ has finished the cat food, and is lapping up the water. You wish you had some milk. There is some at home. Perhaps you should take _____ in for good? 'Keep me company. But what would the landlord think?'

Looking after _____ could get your mind off the funeral, at least. 'Keep busy. That's the way to stop thinking about death.' (You're starting to sound like your father again.)

But a nagging thought comes. 'Every time I see _____ I'll think of Aunt Jane. And that black colour reminds me of bad luck, and dying.' Perhaps keeping _____ isn't such a good idea after all.

How do you feel?

1 *'I need to keep busy, and get my mind off death.'* (**turn to page 46**)
2 *'Great! _____ will be good to have around to remind me of Aunt Jane, especially as the funeral gets near. I think I do want to go to it now.'* (**turn to page 17**)
3 *'I feel uncertain still. Better ring Pete.'* (**turn to page 11**)
4 *'_____ is starting to give me the creeps.'* (**turn to page 27**)

Suffering is a difficult issue. But would everything be all right if people didn't suffer? Some people say it improves your character, or helps you write deep poetry.

You're not too impressed. 'It's hard to think of Aunt Jane in pain, dying. Much easier to think of her happy and laughing. Or even just being normal. And it's not only my aunt,' you think. 'Lots of people suffer.'

Well, you're right. People do get sick and die all the time. Sometimes it's in tragic circumstances. Innocent people are robbed or killed, even at football matches. The world is full of pointless wars. Mass suffering can be caused by human error. Safety standards are ignored, or mistakes made through tiredness or stress.

Sometimes suffering is from natural causes. Earthquakes, drought, floods or fires. We can see and hear the misery on TV every day. Yet it's only when we're faced with it personally that we're actually touched by it. Most of us live as if all this suffering didn't exist.

Getting depressed? Or bothered? Or angry?

Do you want to:

1 *Leave God out of it altogether? 'I don't want to know a God who allows evil to happen.'* (**turn to page 62**)
2 *Find out what Aunt Jane thought about suffering?* (**turn to page 63**)

Aunt Jane didn't have much time for the devil, or evil. You realize that because of the sharp way she reacted to Kate's ideas. But that wasn't very often. She much preferred to talk about Jesus.

'Kate, you're playing with fire!' she'd tell her. 'Open yourself to spirits and you're letting evil get a hold in your life. We're selfish enough as it is without getting help from anywhere else!'

Pretty fierce she'd get. She never seemed to hold a grudge against Kate, though she got angry at her ideas. It was as if she got angry because she cared about her.

Kate once asked her 'Why do you get so upset about it?'

Aunt Jane said something about Jesus having freed her from such things. 'I went off the rails when I was young, and got in with a bad crowd. Jesus helped me see the mess I was getting into, and helped me out of it.' She said Jesus had died for her, like someone rescuing her from drowning.

Apparently this Jesus actually used to cast spirits out of people. 'Sounds like the film "The Exorcist",' you think. 'That was creepy.'

Yet Aunt Jane never spoke about Jesus as if he were creepy. 'Jesus loved people out of evil, didn't scare them to bits.'

'This is getting a bit deep,' you think.

1 *You're still curious about Kate.* (**turn to page 45** – *but you might find yourself going round in circles!*)

2 *You want to get on to the funeral.* (**turn to page 60**)

3 *Your doubts about going to the funeral are growing. A wreath sounds a better idea.* (**turn to page 8**)

'My aunt might have believed in God. I don't. We don't need to invent a God,' you think.

'Doesn't religion cause all the trouble in the world? Fighting in Lebanon and Israel, trouble between India and Pakistan, terrorism in Northern Ireland and Sri Lanka and so on.'

Perhaps you believe in *people*, rather than any gods? In that case, you are a 'secular humanist'. God-freaks believe in people too. They get the idea from God. God believes in people. So they're 'religious humanists'. Of course, they don't always live like it.

Perhaps you're about ready to give up on this book. (If you really care about people, you won't mind if you've missed the gratuitous sex and violence.)

But, please realize that you – and the world – are on your own, given what you believe. You're saying 'I am the only one who can say what life is about.'

We wish you well. And good luck. We think you'll need it. Can people be depended on to be fair, loving, honest, caring?

Of course, you could do some more looking around. How about one of these questions?

1 *Do you know the basic facts about Jesus?* (**If not, turn to page 39**)

2 *How do we know if God exists?* (**turn to page 40**)

3 *What did Aunt Jane think of God?* (**turn to page 53**)

4 *You might want to think a bit more about life without God.* (**turn to page 44**)

What's a hypocrite?

Someone who wears a mask pretending to be something they aren't. Being false. Some people dress up in nice clothes on a Sunday and go to church and pretend that they don't lie and act selfishly the rest of the week. That's hypocrisy.

Some people will go to Aunt Jane's funeral and smile or cry and say how much they loved her when they didn't care enough to visit her even when she was dying. That's hypocrisy.

Some people, if they are honest, will realize that we are all a little hypocritical. That's Aunt Jane. 'I'm not perfect, just forgiven.' That was her line.

'Does that mean God can forgive even you for being a hypocrite?' Aunt Jane seemed to think so.

What do you think?

1 *'Did my aunt just believe in God so she could get rid of her guilt feelings?'* (**turn to page 25**)
2 *'I'd like to know more about this forgiveness you can get for being such a hypocrite.'* (**turn to page 53**)
3 *'I don't want to be a hypocrite. I'd like to do something practical. I'll give a donation to Cancer Research in memory of Aunt Jane.'* (**turn to page 59**)
4 *'You Christians are always talking about sin, and stopping the fun.'* (**turn to page 64**)

Oh dear, oh dear, oh dear! You seem to have great difficulty in making decisions. Or maybe not. It's hard to be sure.

But time is running out and a choice has to be made. It is clear that something holds you back from being decisive. Perhaps your mother dropped you on your head when you were a baby. Maybe you just want to go along with the crowd, but you don't know where the crowd's going.

It might be the fact of death itself that is making this decision so hard. To realize that your aunt is dead means realizing that you also will die one day.

That's not a pleasant thought, is it? Becoming a lump of dead flesh. Most of us worry, 'What will happen to me as a person?' Let's face it, we're all scared of dying.

How do you deal with your fears?

1 *Ignore them and get on with living.* (**turn to page 42**)
2 *Talk to someone about them. Have a drink with your brother in the pub.* (**turn to page 38**)
3 *Your aunt would have prayed about it. So you decide to try it.* (**turn to page 48**)
4 *You've made a firm decision to face your fears.* (**turn to page 47**)

(turn to page 42)
(turn to page 38)
(turn to page 48)
(turn to page 47)

It takes some time with the phone book but in the end you find the only minister it could be. You pick up the phone. It's not an easy call to make.

A voice answers. You say something about your aunt and the funeral. 'Yes, that's right, I'm taking Jane's funeral' the voice replies. 'How can I help you?'

(Sounds fairly normal actually, perhaps a little embarrassed. It seems he doesn't find talking about death easy either.)

You feel you need to talk. You begin to ask some tentative questions. Where to sit, what time to get there. After a few minutes the minister suggests it might be good to meet and have a chat. 'Any afternoon after about four you'll find me home. I'd be happy to see you,' he ends.

You're a bit uncertain about seeing him. 'I know I want to go to the funeral now,' you think. 'But do I want to talk with the minister?'

You decide:

1 *Just to go to the funeral, and say 'Hello' there.* (**turn to page 60**)
2 *You will go round for a chat.* (**turn to page 50**)

Saying goodbyes. You remember the happiest one of your life (so far anyway). It was when you set off on your one and only holiday abroad. You had something to look forward to, and felt terrific.

You also remember the worst farewell. It was when Pete cleared out from home to live with Kate. You'd just had a fight with him, Kate had turned on her witchy act and you felt wretched.

Well, Aunt Jane's gone now. 'Don't really know where to. Probably nowhere at all. Dad would say this life is all we have,' you think. 'Anyway what matters is being brave about life without others.'

Your aunt might not have agreed. 'Can't live for yourself' she'd say. 'You'll end up dying by yourself.' Yet she'd cried at old Reg's funeral. Said she was sure he was safe in God's hands now, but was still sorry to lose him.

You're starting to focus your ideas now. You decide to:

1 *Just get on with living, funeral or not.* (**turn to page 42**)
2 *Go to the funeral still, but have nothing to do with the religious bits.* (**turn to page 32**)
3 *Think about where Aunt Jane might be now.* (**turn to page 22**)

You are an honest person, at least. A lot of people wouldn't admit that they use alcohol to solve their problems.

Of course, alcohol doesn't solve the problems. It just helps you forget. Well, it helps you forget for the time being. Well, OK, let's face it, alcohol actually causes more problems.

Still, a drink would be nice right now. But remember what Dad said, 'Never drink alone.'

Will you:

1 *Drink that six-pack all by yourself?*
OK. Close this book now. Start it again tomorrow when you're sober. But we hope you'll at least turn to page 39 to find out something about Jesus. He was good with heavy drinkers.

2 *Meet your brother for a drink at the pub?* (**turn to page 38**)

3 *Forget the booze and think about Aunt Jane's attitude to life.* (**turn to page 14**)

The pub is about half full. You get a drink, and find a table with a spare seat. Some people are sitting only three or four feet away. Makes you a bit self-conscious. Then Pete walks in.

'Hi, Pete. Long time no see.' He sits down. 'Can I get you a drink?'

He looks like he's put away a few already. But he accepts your offer. You get a refill, too. Perhaps a few drinks will help. You drink in silence for a bit.

'Well, are you going or not?' Pete asks. Then he suddenly blurts out, 'I used to love Aunt Jane, but she drove Kate up the wall. Kate sure doesn't want to go. Says churches upset her.'

You'd hoped Pete wouldn't bring up Kate. Aunt Jane didn't approve of her dabbling in the occult. The fight you'd had with Pete had been over Kate, too. His words make you defend your aunt.

'I thought Aunt Jane was OK. She didn't want to hurt Kate. She was the first family member to have her round to tea, remember. Mum couldn't cope with the idea, and Dad was just too busy as usual. I reckon you owe it to her to go.'

'Might do me good to say goodbye I suppose,' Pete grunts. 'The whole business makes me feel miserable. Why should she have to die from cancer? I thought she was religious. You just can't trust anything these days.'

He gets another round of drinks. Both of you are feeling a bit teary. You blow your nose a few times. The people next to you decide they've finished their drink. You're left to yourselves.

Pete puts his arm around you. 'Thash the way. Cry 'tout. Goo' bawl'll 'elp.'

His slurred words make you stop. He's getting drunk, but you want to talk. Couldn't he wait at least until after the funeral for the wake?

(***Please turn to page 52.*** *Talks in pubs usually take a while!*)

Christians believe that the best way to know God, in fact the only way, is through Jesus Christ.

Jesus lived in the country of Israel about 2,000 years ago. For the last three years of his life, when he was about thirty years old, he went around teaching people, healing them, and doing amazing things. He gathered a group of followers who came to believe he was someone special.

Jesus became a threat to the powers that be, both in politics and religion. So he was lynched. Crucified actually. Yet, three days later, his followers were going around saying that God had raised him from the dead.

These first Christians believed his death had somehow dealt with everything they had wrong with them. It had brought them back to being friends with God. They certainly knew it made a difference. They experienced God's forgiveness for all that was wrong with them. It was like having a big load lifted off you.

They called it all 'Good News'. Christians have been talking about it ever since. That was what Aunt Jane was on about.

You think about this for a bit.

1 *'This story comes from the Bible. How can I be sure the Bible got its facts straight?'* (**turn to page 79**)
2 *'So what? Jesus existed. Maybe even rose from the dead. But what's that got to do with me?'* (**turn to page 69**)
3 *'Christians might think they have good news. But they're so boring! Pray all the time and never have any fun.'* (**turn to page 81**)

PS You can read the unabridged version of the story of Jesus for yourself in the Bible. See the sections by Matthew, Mark, Luke or John. (Mark's is the shortest!)

We hope you don't expect to discover in five minutes flat whether God exists or not! After all, if we could get a handle on God in only five minutes, we wouldn't have much of a God, would we?

Who needs a God no bigger than your little mind?

On the other hand, ask yourself, 'What would I like God to *do* to prove he exists?'

Aunt Jane used to like the film 'Oh God!', starring George Burns as God. (If you haven't seen it, do. It's quite funny, and you won't have to worry about getting brainwashed.) God was in a bit of a quandary. How could people be convinced today that God really existed? He did all sorts of miracles. But they didn't work on anyone except the hero in the story, John Denver!

Do you really want to hear a voice from heaven? Personally, we think we'd die of fright.

And anyway, just to prove that God exists wouldn't tell you what God is like. Who wants to get in touch with one of those wham-bam-thank-you-mam gods the old pagans believed in? Nasty types, they were. Either power-hungry rapists or drunks, or a bit of both.

Christians believe that Jesus is the best guide to God.

What do you think?

1 *'I want to find out more about my aunt's sort of God.'* (**turn to page 53**)
2 *'I'd better learn a bit about this Jesus.'* (**turn to page 39**)
(turn to page 53)
(turn to page 39)

Welcome to God's family! It has members from just about every place there is. Including heaven. That's where your aunt is now. She's still part of God's family, but not bothered by the problems of this life.

You'll want to meet other members of God's family. Some will be friendly. Others will be worried about their problems. Some might be a bit wary of a newcomer like you. You may be wary of them too! A bit like meeting a distant cousin paying a first visit. (Hopefully they'll be easier to get on with than Randolph!)

You may already know where God's family meets near you. Give your local minister a ring. Maybe the church has a notice board with meeting-times on it. Or drop around one Sunday morning about 10 o'clock. Something should be happening at around that time.

You'll want to know more about your new friend, Jesus, too. His story is told in the Bible. You can get a copy at your local church, bookshop, or library. We suggest you start with the *Good News Bible*.

The Bible is a big book. A good place to start is three-quarters through, with a section called 'Mark'. You can get help reading it from groups like Scripture Union. They're in the phone book.

Now you've started, remember two things. One, *keep* praying! Share all your life with God – good and bad. Two, God wants you in his family as an active member. Don't be selfish with God's love. Share it around.

Enjoy loving and serving God.

We hope you will want to choose all the new options below. But you'll have to start with just one.

1 *You're ready to go to the funeral now. It might feel different now that you're part of God's family.* (**turn to page 60**)
2 *Don't think that suddenly all your problems have been solved. You've lots of questions to explore.* (**turn to page 77**)
3 *You'd like to have a copy of the help-sheet that your aunt's church hands around to new people.* (**turn to page 78**)

'Life has to be lived whether you're afraid or not. It's easier to ignore your fears.'

It's true. Life is worthwhile. You've got a job and you've got good friends. You may even settle down and have a family someday. What more could you want? ('Apart from a bigger car, a bigger house, a bigger TV – with stereo – and a CD player,' we hear you say.)

But, there are moments, after a particularly bad night at the pub, when you are alone in your flat, when your fears are too close and too real to be pushed away.

'There must be more to life than this,' you think.

And you're right. If death is the end of everything, then your life has no meaning. But if death is not the end, what then?

This is a very good question. It's also a very difficult question!

In the light of this, you:

1 *Think 'What the heck', and buy a six-pack of lager to get your mind off it.* (**turn to page 37**)
2 *Decide to think more about the God your aunt used to talk about.* (**turn to page 53**)
3 *Decide to go to the funeral.* (**turn to page 60**)
4 *Ring up Pete and find out what he's doing about the funeral.* (**turn to page 11**)
5 *Think, 'Nonsense. I'm just a bit depressed. Money for the good life is what really matters.'* (**turn to page 66**)

'Might be better to go to a seance instead of the funeral,' you think. 'What if an evil spirit gave her cancer?'

Your aunt would have been horrified to think some-one went to a seance because of her. This whole busi-ness is much more scary than black cats and walking under ladders.

You think about Pete's girlfriend, Kate. She read the stars, cooked strange food on certain days each month, and simply *lived* by her horoscope. She even used a tarot-card set before she ran off with Pete, to see if it would bring bad luck.

Aunt Jane caught you and Pete with a ouija board once. She got *really* angry. Said it was dangerous, and could let in evil influences.

Well, that scared you. Especially when she got her Bible and read you some of it. She tried it on Kate, too. Didn't scare her though. But Kate's life has been rather a mess. She jumps from one new fad idea to the next.

Aunt Jane tried to get on with Kate and Pete, but they stayed away. Once you heard them saying some-thing like 'That woman can't be got at easily.' You asked Aunt Jane about that. She laughed. Thought it quite funny. Said 'Jesus looks after those who love him. The occult isn't worth the effort. Just stay away from it.'

'I'm being silly,' you think. 'Of course my aunt couldn't have died just because of walking under a ladder. It's at least ten years since she did that anyway.'

But it's got you thinking:

1 *'Why did Aunt Jane have to suffer?'* (**turn to page 30**)
2 *'Why did Aunt Jane get angry about ouija boards and Kate's fads?'* (**turn to page 31**)
3 *Kate was interesting to you. You'd like to know more about her ideas.* (**turn to page 45**)

PS The parts of the Bible that your aunt read you were probably Deuteronomy 18:9–14 and Ephesians 6:10–14.

'Wasn't that a bit unfair to give secular humanism only one page? I feel rather cheated. What about the achievements of socialism? Marx? Freud? Science?' you think.

Wow! You're a heavy thinker.

There *are* lots of good ideas around outside religious circles. And some ideas inside religious circles are wrong, dangerous, deceptive and even idiotic! We admit it! Feel better?

You remember the pride you felt, the sense of real togetherness, at the 'Rock against Racism' concert a year or two back. 'Didn't that show people can do something together without needing to bring God into it?' you ask. 'Haven't the churches always opposed new ideas, like science? And tried to keep the workers in their place?'

OK, there's some truth in that. On the other hand, Christians have been leaders in putting forward many ideas that have made changes possible. Socialism without God seems to turn into dictatorship pretty quickly. Look at China.

Science can end up inventing better ways to kill people, or produce chemicals we can't dispose of. Industry seems to have made a good job of polluting the world. The churches, with others, have often questioned such developments.

These are big issues. Rather beyond this book. But you'd like to think a little more about religion and:

1 *Psychology* (**turn to page 25**)
2 *Science* (**turn to page 56**)
3 *Politics* (**turn to page 9**)

If you're not into this heavy stuff, turn back to page 32 and make another choice.

Or you may be heartily fed up with this book. You think it's hopelessly wrong.

Don't even bother to turn to page 1 again. Just dispose of it. In a non-polluting manner please. Goodbye.

Kate might be interesting, but this book isn't going to help you learn about the occult in any way! Christians don't write off the occult, though, and say it doesn't exist. Like Aunt Jane, they believe the spirit world is dangerous, corrupted.

Getting interested in the devil never did anyone any good.

You:

1 *Give up on this book now. It's too narrow-minded about some things.*

But if you do give up now, we hope you realize that the occult must be pretty important to you.

2 *Learn what Aunt Jane thought about the devil, if you haven't already done so.* (**turn to page 31**)

3 *Decide you're not interested in any sort of superstition, religion included. You just want to get on with living.* (**turn to page 42**)

4 *Decide you* do *want to go to the funeral after all. Some prayers mightn't be such a bad idea.* (**turn to page 60**)

5 *Decide you* don't *want to go. It's all superstition. But a wreath might be a nice idea instead.* (**turn to page 8**)

If the devil is bothering you, try reading C. S. Lewis's book *The Screwtape Letters* (Collins).

If you've been caught up in the occult, we suggest you turn to page 57 and pray the prayer. Without delay.

'It's when you're by yourself you start to think too hard.' That's what Dad always said anyway. 'Only got so many days, you know. Got to fill 'em up. Use what you've got, see?'

Well, he certainly did that. If it wasn't work it was bowls, or the garden club, or watching a game, or fiddling with his car, or having a drink (*'never* alone', he used to say). Kept him happy for a few years, but you wonder what really made him tick.

It was when he had the heart turn that things changed. For six months he had to sit at home with no-one there for hours. Couldn't rush around like he used to. At least he had time to talk. Sad thing was he didn't have much to talk about. At least, nothing that mattered.

'Nothing wrong with being *useful*,' Aunt Jane would say to him. 'But it's who you *are*, Charlie, that matters.'

You start thinking about the two of them. Bit of a contrast!

What do you think?

1 *'I should go to the funeral after all.'* (***turn to page 17***)
2 *'I haven't rung Pete yet.'* (***turn to page 11***)
3 *'A busy life suits me fine. I just want to get on with it.'* (***turn to page 42***)
4 *'Maybe Aunt Jane had a point. I'd like to think more about the way she lived.'* (***turn to page 14***)

(turn to page 17), (turn to page 11), (turn to page 42), (turn to page 14)

Somehow Aunt Jane never seemed afraid of death. Even that last time you saw her, when she knew she was dying, she seemed quiet and peaceful. As if she knew where she was going.

In fact, now you think of it, she said something about it once, when her friend Reg from church died. 'He's gone to be with Jesus.'

You didn't understand at the time. You were only young. Perhaps it's clearer now. Your aunt knew she was going to be with Jesus. So even in her pain she was not afraid.

Everyone dies. It's only while we're alive that we have the choice to prepare for death. Once it has happened, it's too late! Our decision has been made.

What do you think?

1 *'Death is the end, and that's all.'* (**turn to page 32**)
2 *'We can't know for sure about things like death and God.'* (**turn to page 51**)
3 *'I'd like to find out more about how Jesus can help me.'* (**turn to page 69**)

You want some privacy. You check the front door is locked. You pull down the blinds, go into your bedroom and shut the door. You try to kneel but it's too uncomfortable. You sit on the edge of the bed, and start to pray. 'Um, er, um . . . ?'

What do you call a God who might not even be there?

After trying several combinations, you finally settle for 'Ourfatherinheaven', from a vague memory of a prayer Aunt Jane often used.

You think you hear a noise. 'Was that a knock on the door?' You begin again. 'Er, um, Ourfatherinheaven.'

Blushing with embarrassment you continue.

'I don't really, um, know if you're there, sort of, but well, you know Aunt Jane? Er, she didn't seem to be that frightened about dying, but you know, I am, really, in a word, frightened. So if you are there, could you um, well, do something about it? Please?'

You breathe a sigh of relief and wait.

Nothing happens. 'Of course! I forget to end it properly,' you think.

'Amen,' you add in a loud voice.

Still nothing happens.

You feel let down. A bit disappointed. So you decide to have a bath. But just as you are getting well lathered, you realize that you don't feel quite so afraid anymore. Somehow you feel a little comforted.

Because of this you decide:

1   *'I'll go to Aunt's funeral, after all.'* (**turn to page 17**)
2   *'I'll ring Pete to see what he's doing.'* (**turn to page 11**)
3   *'I want to find out more about "Ourfatherinheaven".'* (**turn to page 53**)
4   *'I'll go and feed Aunt Jane's cat.'* (**turn to page 13**)

PS Please dry yourself and put on some clothes before you go any further!
PPS You'll find the prayer your aunt used on page 61.

Christmas. A good time for family get-togethers. But you're worried about this year. 'Without Aunt Jane to referee things, will everyone get along?' She had the knack of helping people put aside their dislikes. At least for a few hours.

'She never seemed to get anything out of the Christmas party,' you realize. 'She never got much from us either! We were pretty stingy with the presents. But she didn't seem to really *need* things.'

You remember her saying each year 'Jesus is the best gift.' She made a point of reminding Dad, 'Christmas dinner is really Jesus' birthday party.' (Dad would just grunt and mumble into his plum pudding something like 'Bah! Humbug! Religion is just for emotional cripples.')

You wonder. What is the true 'spirit of Christmas'? Is it just about spending sprees? What about those who feel lonely, not having a family even to fight with? Does 'family' stand for anything beyond just being related?

Sometimes enjoyable things happened at Christmas apart from Aunt Jane. Perhaps they will again. The trouble is that, without her to remind you all about Jesus, you can't be sure.

You decide you'd like to know more about :

1   *Aunt Jane's ideas about God.* (**turn to page 53**)
2   *This Jesus whose birthday is kept each Christmas.* (**turn to page 39**)
3   *Dad's ideas.* (**turn to page 25**)

Saturday afternoon. You're free, and you hope the minister is, too. You finally make it to the front door, having escaped being mown over by a young dare-devil charging down the drive on a skate board.

You just catch what he says. 'Looking for the minister? Dad's inside. Watching the football.'

The minister guy is OK. You don't know whether he's trying to make you feel at home, or whether he just wants to see the game to the end. But you get through two biscuits and a drink before the final whistle. He asks you to call him Bill, but you feel easier with Mr Purdue.

It doesn't take long to go through the arrangements for the funeral. The minister doesn't seem to mind your questions. You now have a much better idea of what will happen and what is expected of you.

Much to your surprise you feel quite relaxed. Here you are, sitting in a minister's house, slumped in a chair helping yourself to biscuits. You never imagined you'd feel at home in such a situation.

You decide that now might be a good time to ask some questions that are puzzling you.

1 *'Why are there so many different churches?'* (**turn to page 76**)
2 *'Aren't all religions really the same underneath?'* (**turn to page 70**)
3 *'How come you're interested in football, Mr Purdue? Aren't Christians supposed to pray all the time?'* (**turn to page 81**)
4 *'Can we talk some more about Aunt Jane?'* (**turn to page 67**)

PS You may have lots of other questions to ask. Try page 77 if you'd like to find out where some are discussed in this book.

OK, so you've decided you can't know whether or not God exists. In that case, you're an agnostic. (The word means a person who is a 'not-knower'.)

You first heard the word from cousin Randolph. 'Personally, I'm an agnostic,' he announced one Christmas dinner. You realize now that was an odd thing for Randolph to say. He would normally never admit there was something he didn't know.

Many people call themselves agnostics. Sometimes it is after a lot of hard thinking and searching. (Sometimes it's to *avoid* all the hard thinking and searching!)

Some agnostics would like to believe in God, but feel they can't do so in all honesty. Others are unwilling to believe in God. They know that their lives would have to change as a result of such belief.

So how do agnostics get on with living? Mostly they're not much different from anyone else. Some struggle hard to make a useful life. Some don't really have definite opinions about anything, since there is no way of being really sure what is good or bad.

Do you live as if you were sure about what is right and wrong? If so, what makes you sure?

Christians recognize that there's lots they don't know (including things about God). Faith doesn't mean you know or understand everything. It's a gift from God, who can see the whole picture. Our job is to trust God, and act on what he shows us is true.

What do you think?

1 *'I'm quite happy to be an agnostic. Let me get to the funeral and get it over with.'* (**turn to page 60**)

2 *'Perhaps there is a God. Can you prove it?'* (**turn to page 40**)

3 *'I can live without God, thank you.'* (**turn to page 32**)

4 *'I'm quite happy as I am. But I'm getting sick of this book, harping on about religion.'* Sorry! We suggest you send it to the paper-recyclers, or give it to someone you want to annoy.

You start to think aloud. 'I was just thinking of her old treasure box. She used to tell such good stories about the things we'd find in it.'

Pete suddenly smiles. 'The besht one wassat gory story 'bout nails,' he says. You remember it well.

You'd found them at the bottom of the box. Long, rusty, square rather than round. Pete had made up some story of how they'd been used to torture people. You didn't like that, and ran to Aunt Jane.

'Well he would say something like that,' she'd said. You were relieved. 'They're some old nails from my grandad's place. But they remind me of someone who was tortured with nails. Jesus.' That quite shocked you. Wasn't this Jesus all nice and good? So why was he tortured? Pete was all ears by now.

'Jesus was killed by being nailed up on a tree,' Aunt Jane explained. Pete thrilled with horror. It just made you feel sick. 'It was because people couldn't stand his goodness. His dying took away my badness,' she went on. 'But Jesus didn't stay dead. God brought him to life again. That's why he is my friend now.'

Pete burps. You come back from your dreaming. Jesus must have meant a lot to Aunt Jane if she thought he'd died for her. Bit like being rescued by someone.

Pete has put his head on the bar. Nodding off. You shake his shoulder. 'Wake up, stupid. What would Aunt Jane think? Are we going or not?'

Pete snores on. You're left to decide for yourself. But it has been good to talk about your aunt, and a few tears did no harm. What do you want to do?

1 *'I'd like to talk some more with someone a bit more helpful. The minister sounds as good as anyone.'* (**turn to page 50**)
2 *'I'm going to the funeral, Pete or not.'* (**turn to page 60**)
3 *'I'd like to hear some more about this Jesus Aunt Jane talked about.'* (**turn to page 39**)

Aunt Jane believed in God. She not only believed that God existed. She also prayed to him. Believed God loved her just as she was.

In fact, this God is the one that Christians believe in. The God who knows everything there is to know about you, but loves you just the same.

The God who made the whole universe but who is concerned for every little corner of the creation. Including your corner.

The God who could click his fingers and get rid of all the problems in the world, but prefers to get his hands dirty by being involved with us. With you.

'But why don't Christians act as if they really believed God was like that?' you think. 'They can make God sound so far away. Or scary. Or just plain boring.'

Well, as Aunt Jane used to say, 'Christians aren't perfect, just forgiven.' She'd laugh, 'I'm not looking for the perfect church, because if I join it it won't be perfect any more!'

What now? Here are some suggestions:

1 *If you haven't already found out who Jesus is, we think that now is a good time to do so.* (**turn to page 39**)
2 *If you haven't read the 'Good News' leaflet, perhaps you should.* (**turn to page 57**)
3 *Or you could set out for the funeral. Hopefully feeling grateful for all Aunt Jane meant to you.* (**turn to page 60**)

SEX & VIOLENCE

STEAMY SEX IN SURGERY

'I LIVED IN SIN'

EXPOSED STAR IN SEX SCANDAL

Headlines like these grab your attention, don't they? People love to read juicy bits like this. So we thought you'd manage to find this page without help from us.

'Now how about some violence?' you ask.

That's a bit harder. Sex is something good. God likes it. God invented it! So it can be OK to have a laugh about it sometimes. Violence is something else. It isn't very funny, in any situation. Not even in cartoons.

What really worries us is that some people fill their heads with this sort of stuff every day of the week. Magazines. Books. Movies. Videos. Heads like that need more than cleaning out. They need a complete overhaul.

If violence is your ultimate idea of fun, you won't get a lot out of reading this book. We hope you'll get the point and go on to something more constructive. Make peace not war.

What do you think?

1 *'Christians just can't handle sex.'* (**turn to page 71**)
2 *'Why do Christians always spoil the fun? You'll start talking about sin in a minute.'* (**turn to page 64**)
3 *'I'll head for the pub to meet Pete. He's more interesting than you lot.'* (**turn to page 38**)

You probably have an idea of God sitting on a big throne and judging us when we die. As each person comes up, God gives the thumbs up (because they're pretty good), or the thumbs down (because they're pretty bad).

This is sort of right. But you've got the picture twisted. According to the Bible, you can't get into heaven by being good. On the other hand, you don't end up in hell just because of a few cigarettes behind the bike shed at school.

Judgment is more to do with the whole pattern of your life. The sorts of decisions you've made because of who you are.

If you've spent your life choosing not to be with God, then that's the way it will be for ever. God will underline your decision. And that'll be hell. (It would be pretty mean of God to force you to live with him for ever, if you didn't want God around for your seventy years or so on earth!)

Aunt Jane's aim in life was to live for God. 'If you trust God and live with him now, then God can be trusted to live with you for ever.'

Perhaps being without God doesn't sound too bad. But think about your life as it is now, going on for ever and ever, without God. Does it really sound all that wonderful? People like your aunt won't be around with you. They'll be with God. You'll be left with the rest. Including Randolph. For ever.

All this serious stuff means that:

1   *'I want to know more about this God.'* (**turn to page 53**)

2   *'I'm still not sure if God exists or not.'* (**turn to page 40**)

3   *'I don't want to think about this any more. I'll just get through the funeral.'* (**turn to page 60**)

PS The Bible has lots of examples of Jesus asking people to decide where their lives were heading. Try Mark 10:17–31, or Matthew 25. And especially John 3:1–21.

Has science disproved religion?

If you mean, 'Hasn't psychology explained away religion as just feelings?' then you are partly right. We have learnt a lot about human nature from psychologists. Perhaps you should turn to page 25.

If you mean 'Haven't geology and physics explained how the world was made?' then you're partly right. We have learnt a lot about the world from science.

Remember that science teacher from your school days? He managed to enjoy his science *and* help run the Christian Union at lunchtime. He didn't seem to have any problem being a scientist and a Christian at the same time.

He'd say something like this:

Science can only go so far. It describes the physical aspects of our existence. It can help us learn *how* the world got here. It can't tell us *who* made it. Or *why* it is here. Or *how* we should live.

It can tell us what will happen if we mistreat the world. But it can't answer questions like 'Why shouldn't I just enjoy myself now and go on destroying the ozone layer? It's not my problem.'

It can tell us how to split the atom. But it can't tell us how to change human nature so we aren't always trying to blow each other off the face of the earth.

What do you think?

1 *'How can we know whether God exists or not?'* (**turn to page 40**)
2 *'I don't care about bombs and ozone layers. I just want to go to the funeral and get it over with.'* (**turn to page 60**)
3 *'I can get on all right by myself, thank you very much. I don't need religion.'* (**turn to page 32**)

GOOD NEWS

1 *God made everything there is, including you.*
2 *That gives God the right to run your life.*
3 *None of us accepts this. We keep God out of our lives. That leads to trouble and eventually death.*
4 *God sent Jesus to win us back and give us life again.*
5 *Because of Jesus you can pray to God and know his life in your life.*

A prayer:
Thanks, God, for sending Jesus. I know my life is full of death and wrong. I am sorry. Help me to live for you. Amen.

You read through the leaflet. What do you make of it?

1 *'It's really put me off religion. You'll never get me in church, even for a funeral. I'll send some flowers instead.'* (**turn to page 8**)
2 *'It's really put me off religion, but I'll go to the funeral anyway, to say goodbye.'* (**turn to page 36**)
3 *'I feel like throwing it away and this book with it.'* (Please re-cycle both in a non-polluting manner.)
4 *'Why do Christians always go on about sin?'* (**turn to page 64**)
5 *'I'd like to know more about this Jesus.'* (**turn to page 39**)
6 *'It doesn't answer all my problems. Has this book anything to say about my other thirty questions?'* (**turn to page 77**)
7 *'I'd like to pray the prayer.'* (Please do so. **Then turn to page 41.**)

You feel really bad about saying that Aunt Jane was 'just a relative'. She was close to you, more like a friend.

Why do you always want to please other people regardless? You remember your aunt saying 'Be yourself. Don't jump into the fire just because someone tells you to.' She really would not have approved of this wreath business!

She was rarely at a loss in difficult situations. Even when her neighbour's husband died. She would cry, but she would still keep on helping.

What made her so strong? Can you keep running away from thinking about death?

You decide:

1 *'It doesn't help to think all these morbid thoughts. I just want to get back to ordinary living.'* (**turn to page 42**)
2 *'I ought to think about all that religious stuff. It makes me feel uncomfortable, but it made Aunt Jane so strong.'* (**turn to page 14**)
3 *'I think I'll just go to the funeral.'* (**turn to page 60**)
4 *'I'm going to look into this "death" thing once and for all.'* (**turn to page 47**)

You're the practical type. 'I can't stand people who go on and on about a problem yet never get off their butts to do something about it.'

Aunt Jane would be pleased to know about your donation to Cancer Research. That's a good, unselfish sort of thing to do. Help others in her memory. A gift that will last longer than a wreath. But she'd probably appreciate a wreath, too. Didn't she enjoy being given flowers?

Then your Dad comes to mind. He'd certainly never send a wreath – unless it saved him more money than going to the funeral! That's where you get your practical streak from.

What do you think?

1 'Life is better if you keep yourself busy.' (**turn to page 46**)
2 'I can get on living a life that is useful without God.' (**turn to page 32**)
3 'I'd like to do something practical, like feeding my aunt's cat.' (**turn to page 13**)
4 'Dad's right. Saving money is important.' (**turn to page 66**)

The funeral is arranged for 11 a.m. at St Mark's. 'Good,' you think, 'that's easy enough to find.'

Your Mum phoned earlier to check what you'd be wearing. At least she didn't remind you to bring a hankie!

Sandy, your friend at work, said not to to worry. 'Funerals only take half an hour and the minister and undertaker tell you what to do. You'll be alright.'

Still, you're glad to walk up to the door of St Mark's and see Kate and Pete waiting outside. 'Hi,' says Kate, stubbing out a cigarette on the path, but not looking at you. She oozes hostile awkwardness. Obviously feels quite out of place at church.

'Nice day to send off Aunt Jane,' mumbles Pete, looking rather uncomfortable in suit and tie. You smile weakly. It seems wrong to look too happy at a funeral.

The minister, Mr Purdue, arrives, smiling broadly. 'What a wonderful day for Jane! You are most welcome in her church,' he says. 'Come in. We've saved seats for the family in the front. John will give you a book. Don't worry about a thing.' But you are worried. The church is filling up. You never knew Aunt Jane had so many friends. It brings a lump to your throat.

You feel tears in your eyes as you walk to the front behind the usher. 'Oh God!' you think. 'Not in front of all these people!' You don't want to embarrass yourself by crying in public. At least you remembered your hankerchief. You slide into the seat next to Mum. Her eyes are full of tears. 'Lend me a hankie, love,' she whispers.

Oh no! You realize you just said 'Oh God!' And in church, too. That must be blasphemy! Oh . . . drat!

What are you thinking now?

1 *'Did God hear me say that? Will I be struck by lightning?'* (**turn to page 68**)

2 *'I wish I hadn't come so soon. I'm not ready for this funeral yet.'* (**turn to page 34**)

3 *'Let's get on with the funeral.'* (**turn to page 72**)

Some parts of a typical funeral service.

*Heavenly Father, in your Son Jesus Christ you have given us
a true faith and a sure hope.*

*Help us to live as those who believe in the communion of
saints, the forgiveness of sins, and the resurrection to eternal
life.*

Through your Son Jesus Christ, our Lord. Amen.

Psalm 23 (in hymn form):

The Lord's my shepherd, I'll not want.
He makes me down to lie
in pastures green, He leadeth me
the quiet waters by.

Yea, though I walk in death's dark vale
yet will I fear none ill.
For thou art with me; and thy rod
and staff me comfort still.

Goodness and mercy all my life
shall surely follow me:
And in God's house for evermore
my dwelling place shall be.

The Lord's Prayer

Our Father in heaven,
hallowed be your name.
Your kingdom come, your will be done
on earth as in heaven.
Give us today our daily bread.
Forgive us our sins
as we forgive those who sin against us.
Lead us not into temptation,
but deliver us from evil.
For the kingdom, the power, and the glory
are yours, now and for ever. Amen.

OK, so you've decided to leave God out of it.

Now what? The suffering is still there. Can you offer any hope or comfort to your aunt's family and friends? Just that she's dead and that we'll all die? She believed she was going to a better place. Was she deceived?

What about the person who suffers? The one with multiple sclerosis? Or the starving African child? If this is all there is for them, is there any justice? Any point in it all? Any meaning to their lives? Any real hope of good things now – let alone in the future?

There *is* a problem of how a loving God could allow evil. Yet a suffering world without a loving God is a much bigger problem. If there's no God, how do we make any sense of pain and suffering?

As Aunt Jane said that time you saw her in hospital, 'I'm all right, dear. I don't mind a bit of pain as long as I know God is here with me.'

If there is no God, why bother to live a good life? Do we even know what a good life is?

'But I do know what's good. I admire good in other people, like Aunt Jane,' you think. 'My life has a meaning. It's worthwhile, even when the going gets tough.'

Could that be because God made you that way?

How do you react to this?

1 *'It's all too much. I'm definitely going to buy that six-pack of lager, and drown my sorrows.'* (**turn to page 37**)
2 *'I'd like to find out more about what Aunt Jane believed about suffering.'* (**turn to page 63**)
3 *'I'm sorry I bothered to read this far in the book. I've had enough.'*
You could try to find the sex and violence page. Those things take some people's minds of suffering.
4 *'I don't believe in God, but I still believe that life is worthwhile.'* (**turn to page 32**)
5 *'Religion is OK if it helps people cope. But I don't need an emotional crutch to face life.'* (**turn to page 25**)

Your aunt knew she didn't have all the answers. 'Only God does. And if he's concerned about everything, we're bound to have a hard job understanding him.'

God does want us to understand as much as we can, though. Shows us his character and his hopes and purposes for us and the world. Especially through Jesus.

But people wouldn't listen to Jesus. They made fun of him. They beat him, and finally strung him up on a tree. Crucified him. Although he was completely innocent of any crime or wrong-doing. Because of what Jesus went through, God understands what it is like to suffer. Christians find that this makes their suffering more bearable. It can even draw us closer to God.

Aunt Jane believed that good could come out of suffering. 'It could change the way we live. Anyone with any heart who saw those poor children on TV couldn't help but be more generous,' she said. 'But that's no excuse for not trying to stop things like famine before they start. Prevention is better than cure!'

Suffering is a bigger problem even than your aunt's cancer. The Bible talks about all creation suffering, waiting to be set free. God doesn't want anybody – or anything – to suffer. Humans spoilt what God made to be good. That's how suffering and death have come about. One day God will finally free the whole world from suffering. This promise gives all sufferers hope for the future.

What do you think?

1 *'I'm still not convinced. All this God business is just talk.'* (**turn to page 32**)
2 *'I'd like to find out more about Jesus.'* (**turn to page 39**)
3 *'I wish I could be sure that God's there.'* (**turn to page 40**)
4 *'I'd like to do something practical in memory of my aunt. I'll send a donation to Cancer Research.'* (**turn to page 59**)

PS The Bible passage referred to is Romans 8:18–25.

'Christians do talk about sin a lot,' you think. 'They go on about what you mustn't do. Don't get drunk. Don't have sex. God will punish you if you have fun!' But actually you were the one who mentioned sin first!

Your mind is really in gear now. 'What a boring life. If you don't have alcohol at a party how can you have fun? If you don't have sex before you're married, how can you tell if you are suited to each other?'

What a pity we always think sin = sex and alcohol!

Actually Aunt Jane didn't talk a lot about sin, sex or alcohol. She did drink a little wine. 'For my stomach's sake,' she would say. 'That's in the Bible.' You remember that she had some at her Christmas parties. She used to tell the story of Jesus making wine at a wedding reception. 'I hope there'll be champagne in heaven,' she'd say with a laugh.

And it wasn't Aunt Jane who got angry when Pete ran off to 'live in sin' with Kate. That was your Mum, annoyed at what the neighbours would think. She seemed more upset when you ate the last slice of cake without offering it around. (She hadn't spotted Randolph gorging himself on his third piece.) 'Selfishness,' she would say, 'that's the real problem with the world. People who think the world revolves around them.'

Is that what sin really is? Selfishness? Let's face it. We're all selfish. So what can we do about it?

1 *What's Jesus done about our selfishness? (**turn to page 39**)*
2 *What can you do about selfishness? (**turn to page 59**)*
3 *If you just want to think about sin, sex and violence, there's a page for you in this book. But we're not going to tell you where it is!*
4 *Do Christians think sex is sin, though? (**turn to page 71**)*

1 *What's Jesus done about our selfishness? (**turn to page 39**)*
2 *What can you do about selfishness? (**turn to page 59**)*
4 *Do Christians think sex is sin, though? (**turn to page 71**)*

PS Your aunt was referring to 1 Timothy 5:23 and John 2:1–13 in the Bible.

'Is it OK for Christians to swear?' you ask. 'What are you supposed to do when you get angry?'

Remember when your aunt helped you build the tree-house years ago? She wasn't too good with hammer and nails. When she hit her thumb really hard, she said something very un-Aunt-Janeish.

But then she apologized and said it was stupid to swear because it showed a lack of intelligent vocabulary.

'What's "a lack of intelligent vocabulary"?' you asked.

'It means you are too stupid to express yourself clearly. So you use a word associated with bodily functions to cover your ignorance,' she primly replied.

(Bodily functions. And sex. And religion. Yes. That does account for most of our swear words. Randolph's for sure. Probably says something about our biggest hang-ups. God, sex, and our own bodies. All the things we need most in life.)

Aunt Jane went on to say, 'I hope I haven't offended you with my lapse in vocabulary.'

'I'm not offended,' you thought. But it was important to Aunt Jane to consider the feelings of others. She wouldn't want to swear in front of others in case it hurt them in some way.

How do you feel?

1 *You're sorry for your 'lack of intelligent vocabulary'. You want to get back to what you were doing when you caught yourself swearing. (If you were at the funeral* **turn to page 60***. Otherwise,* **turn to page 14***.)*

2 *'Maybe religion is just for people with hang-ups,' you think. (****turn to page 25****)*

3 *'Christians and sex don't seem to mix too well. Is sex all right or not?' you want to know. (****turn to page 71****)*

PS If you want to check out what Jesus said, then see Matthew 4:34–37 and 12:36–37.

'Money isn't everything. But it's way ahead of whatever comes in second place!' That's what your Dad would say for a laugh.

Yet, it isn't just a joke. A lot of people live with that as their golden rule. Our whole society is set up to help us spend money. We make money so we can spend it so that we can make some more . . .

Of course, not having enough money makes us very unhappy. Only heartless people would say that it's OK for people to live without basic necessities.

But just having money doesn't seem to make people any happier. Aunt Jane once read you a magazine story on all the big money-winners in lotteries from the past few years. 'No-one was happier because of their big win,' she said. 'In fact, a lot of them found that a pile of money brought them unhappiness, family fights, even divorce.'

She was right, too. Randolph always seems to have pots of money. Enough to make you jealous, anyway. But he nevers seems to be happy with . . . well, with himself.

Christians believe wealth means a lot more than having money. It's to do with having friends, opportunities like education, being content with yourself, having an aim in life. And God at the centre.

What do you think?

1 *'Aunt Jane seemed pretty content with herself. I wonder what her aim in life was.'* (**turn to page 14**)
2 *'I ought to go to the pub and see if I can meet up with some friends there.'* (**turn to page 74**)
3 *'I'd like to go to the funeral. But if they dare to pass around the plate and ask for money, I'll get up and walk out.'* (**turn to page 60**)

Mr Purdue and you chat about Aunt Jane for a bit. You get back to the funeral.

'Did Jane ever tell you about Reg's funeral?' he asks.

'I was there. I was only a kid at the time,' you reply. 'All I remember is that Aunt Jane cried. I never knew Reg well, but she did.'

'Yes, she'd lost a good friend. She missed him.'

('Was there some sort of love affair with Reg?' you wonder.)

Mr Purdue seems to read your thoughts. 'Nothing romantic. Just close friends, especially as Christians. Jane and Reg belonged to God's family. They still do, because Jesus was their friend.'

You think Mr Purdue may be getting around to the religious bit. You're worried he may even break into praying any moment now. But then he tells you he's got to start getting ready for church tomorrow. He gives you a piece of paper at the door.

'This has my address on it, and some readable books you might be interested in.' He shakes your hand. 'I'll see you at the funeral. God bless you.'

'Thanks for the biscuits, and, er, everything,' you say, and leave.

Some bigger issues have started to buzz around your mind. Do you:

1 *Want to think about your aunt's faith?* (**turn to page 14**)

2 *Find yourself wondering about why people suffer?* (**turn to page 30**)

3 *Start reading the paper he's given you?* (**turn to page 78**)

4 *Put the thought of the funeral aside for the moment and head for the pub?* (**turn to page 74**)

Have you committed a terrible sin by exclaiming, 'Oh God!'?

The Ten Commandments do say 'You shall not take the name of the Lord your God in vain.' They put blasphemy in the same class as stealing or murder.

But what exactly *is* blasphemy? If you were God, would you throw a bolt of lightning at someone for using your name just because they got angry or exasperated? Probably not, if you're a half-way decent God. Certainly not, if you're the God of the Bible.

Blasphemy is not just saying certain words at the wrong time and in the wrong place. That's a bit like saying 'Oh Aunt Jane!' when you stub your toe. In one sense, it's only words.

Blasphemy, taking God's name in vain, is a way of life, not just a set of words. It is living your whole life as if God doesn't exist or doesn't matter.

Christians believe that God is real, and has done everything for us. So it's really a terrible thing to live as if that isn't true. It's as if someone loved you so much that they made huge sacrifices for you, and you just shrugged your shoulders and said, 'So what?'

And in this sense a lot of people commit the sin of blasphemy every day of their lives without ever once saying 'Oh God!'

What do you think now?

1 *'What things do Christians claim God has done for us that are so great?'* (**turn to page 57**)
2 *'Does all this mean it is OK to swear, then?'* (**turn to page 65**)
3 *'I'm relieved!'* (If you are at the funeral, **go back to page 60.** Otherwise, **go back to page 14.**)

1 *'What things do Christians claim God has done for us that are so great?'* (**turn to page 57**)
2 *'Does all this mean it is OK to swear, then?'* (**turn to page 65**)
3 *'I'm relieved!'* (If you are at the funeral, **go back to page 60.** Otherwise, **go back to page 14.**)

PS You can find the Ten Commandments in Exodus 20 and Deuteronomy 5, near the beginning of the Bible.

Jesus and his followers lived about 2,000 years ago. What does that have to do with us in the twentieth century? Why do people today talk about the story of Jesus as the 'Good News'?

Some people didn't think Jesus was good news then, and others still don't now.

They said it was no way for God to act, to come and walk around like an ordinary person on earth. Said there was nothing wrong with them anyway, that they didn't need help, or to make friends with God. Said that no-one could come back from the dead.

You might even agree with them.

But for Aunt Jane, it *was* good news. She wasn't afraid of dying, because she believed in a God who could raise her from the dead.

She wasn't a pushy type of person because she believed in a God who doesn't throw his weight around. In fact, she could love other people, even when they mistreated her. She knew God loved her, and that was what really counted.

She had time for other people. She had time for you. Because God had all the time in the world for her.

What do you think?

1 *'I ought to get straight the basic facts about this Good News.'* (**turn to page 57**)
2 *'I want to think some more about the God that Aunt Jane believed in.'* (**turn to page 53**)
3 *'I think I'm ready to set out for the funeral.'* (**turn to page 60**)
4 *'I still can't see what it's all got to do with me. I can get on perfectly well without God.'* (**turn to page 32**)

'Of course, I don't think it matters what we believe, does it,' you begin nervously. 'As long as we're sincere.'

'Really?' says Bill Purdue. 'What a great kick!' he shouts at the TV. 'Sorry. Where were we? Oh yes. What we believe. Does it matter?'

'Yes. I mean, as long as we all worship the same God.'

'Do we?' he asks, settling back in his armchair. 'Do we all worship the same God?'

You're almost sorry you began this conversation. What if he tries to convert you to his religion?

'Well, yes. You know. If people were more tolerant we wouldn't have fighting in Ireland and the Middle East and . . .'

'Wouldn't we?' he responds, glancing at the TV again. Scores from other grounds are coming in.

You are wondering whether to keep trying with this conversation.

What next?

1 *You see your chance to change the topic. Mr Purdue doesn't seem keen on it anyway.* (**turn to page 67**)
2 *This really does bug you about Christianity. Why do Christians think they are right? Bite the bullet and continue the conversation.* (**turn to page 73**)

Christians do often appear to say sex is bad. But the Bible doesn't.

The Bible has quite a lot to say about sex. Not just nasty stories like King David having sex with another man's wife, or his son Amnon raping his sister. On the plus side, there is a whole book of love songs between a man and woman. It is so explicit about sex that some Christians have been embarrassed by it. A few have even tried to pretend it isn't in the Bible.

There's nothing wrong with sex between a man and a woman as an expression of their love, as part of their life-long commitment to each other. In fact, the Bible teaches that they should help each other in their sex life. This is one of the most important sides to marriage.

What *can* be wrong is the way we use sex. It is wrong to use someone else's body just to please yourself. That's why Aunt Jane thought being selfish was the worst sin of all.

This whole topic does sound embarrassing in a way. You don't like speaking of Aunt Jane and sex in the same breath. But it may be due to your hang-ups about sex. She may have had a man in her life. Even a lover! She was human, down-to-earth, after all.

What now?

1 *You wonder, 'Do I have to pray all the time, and live a boring life, to be a Christian?'* (**turn to page 81**)
2 *If you haven't rung your brother Pete for a chat, you probably should.* (**turn to page 11**)
3 *Or you might like to head off to the pub.* (**turn to page 74**)

PS Sex is a big subject. A good book on it is *Life in a Sex-mad Society*, by Joyce Huggett (Frameworks, 1988). PPS The Bible passages mentioned on this page are (in order), 2 Samuel 11 – 13, the Song of Solomon, and 1 Corinthians 7.

The organ starts playing. It's the tune of 'The Lord's my shepherd.' Just about the only hymn you know. (Oh, except for the first verse of 'Amazing Grace', and a few lines of 'Abide with me.')

Whenever you sing 'Amazing Grace' you're at full volume, accompanied in your mind by a large band of Scottish pipers. But 'The Lord's my shepherd' always puts a lump in your throat. You can only whisper it.

Why is this? Does it just remind you of things from the past? Is it because you know the words were true for your aunt? Maybe it's the pictures in it. Sheep by still waters with their caring shepherd.

Or is it something else? The feeling that now 'in death's dark vale' God is more real and close to you?

Much of the service washes by without making any impression on you. The first prayer gets you thinking.

Heavenly Father, in your son Jesus Christ
you have given us a true faith and a sure hope.

You read it a couple of times. Certainly it was true for your aunt. It seems to be true for many in church around you. But what faith and hope do you have?

Your attention starts to wander. You gaze around. To the flowers. To the stained glass windows, with the pools of blue and red they cast on the stone pillars.

But each time your eyes come back to rest on the coffin. There is no getting away from it. Or from death.

What are you feeling?

1 *'Death* is *the end. We just have to face it.'* And that's your final decision. (**turn to page 87**)
2 *'Hymns are just nice sentiments. I'm glad to be able to say goodbye to Aunt Jane in her church. But I don't believe everything that's going on.'* (**turn to page 83**)
3 *'God is with me somehow. Jesus' victory over death is starting to make sense.'* (**turn to page 83**)

'Sorry to be so rude,' he says, turning off the TV. 'Other religions, eh? Tolerance. Mmm. Wouldn't hurt to see some tolerance in Ireland. That's certainly what the churches there want.'

'I agree. After all, we all worship the same God.'

'Do we?' he repeats. 'I mean, Moslems and Buddhists and Hindus and Mormons. They don't really worship the same God as Christians, you know. Not even Jews have the same idea of God, though they're pretty close.'

You think this sounds rather narrow-minded. But he hasn't finished yet.

'Christians reckon Jesus Christ is God. That's why we're called Christ-ians,' he continues. 'Other religions find that pretty offensive. You know, saying that a man was God walking around in the flesh.'

This is about where your knowledge of other religions runs out. Nevertheless, you stumble on, 'But as long as we're all sincere . . .'

The minister cuts you off. 'I see a lot of people in this country sincerely living for themselves. Worshipping money, or pleasure, or even football,' he laughs. 'Doesn't mean they're right, though, does it? Sincerity is nice but it's not everything.'

You're wishing you could just talk about something else. Perhaps the footy.

Mr Purdue is going strong now. 'My soccer team might sincerely believe they've got the ball over the goal line and scored.' (Is he reading your thoughts again?) 'But if it's the wrong goal line, it doesn't matter how sincere they are. They've just scored for the other team.' You start to see his point.

What do you think?

1   *You've really had enough on religions and even enough on football.* (**turn to page 67**)
2   *This minister makes a lot of sense. You want to ask more questions.* (**turn back to page 50 and choose another**)

The pub is crowded. The band is already in action. Saturday means they're loud. You feel a bit lonely, cut off. Then you spot Sandy with some friends. Hasn't been around for ages, since the operation.

'Hi!' you yell. 'You're looking great!'

'Must have been my lucky day when brain tumours were handed out,' Sandy shouts back. 'No sign of it now.'

The band finishes its number. You get a drink, and a refill for Sandy.

'I suppose you *were* lucky. Didn't the operation and therapy do most of the good though?' you ask.

'Guess so. I sure hated it all,' replies Sandy. 'But I still put it down to good luck mostly.'

'Tonight might be your lucky night on the slot machines,' someone comments. 'First night back in the pub!'

Sandy agrees, and heads for the row of gambling machines. 'Join me? Gotta be in it to win it!'

You haven't finished your drink, so stay with the others for a chat. Then the band starts up again. You like their work, but after an hour feel a headache coming on.

You decide:

1 *'I'll have a go on the machines after all.'* (**turn to page 82**)

2 *'I've stayed long enough at the pub. I'll head home for a quiet Sunday before the funeral.'* (**turn to page 60**)

3 *'I feel like a solid booze-up. It's the best way to forget my problems.'* (**turn to page 37**)

A lot of ideas run round your head.

'Is life all a matter of chance? God sitting up in heaven dealing the cards, and sometimes it comes up aces for you? You win some, you lose some. Is God there at all? Is life simply a random event? Don't the scientists say everything just happened?'

Not very satisfactory ideas, are they? There's no point in life if it's all just luck. You might as well lie down and die. Or let it all wash over you.

Of course, most of us don't live as if life were pure chance. We assume a fair degree of cause and effect. Every time you push the 'on' button your radio starts blasting. (Or you need new batteries. Or a repair job!)

If you drink too much and drive too fast, you're asking for trouble. But not always. You might arrive home no worse for wear, yet cause an accident for someone driving carefully and fully sober. Any luck involved is helped along an awful lot by your stupid behaviour.

But good people like Aunt Jane do get cancer and die.

God doesn't promise a rose garden for Jesus' followers. After all, Jesus himself was tortured to death.

What makes more sense? That life is only a matter of chance? Or that there is a pattern to life, even if we don't understand it all?

Christians believe that only God can see the whole picture. And that God can even work through what seems random to us.

What do you think?

1 *'It still bothers me. How can God allow suffering?'* (**turn to page 30**)

2 *'Drinking is a problem for me.'* (**turn to page 37**)

3 *'Science is all we need. It's disproved God.'* (**turn to page 56**)

'Why are there so many churches?' you think. 'Anglicans, Baptists, Catholics . . . Some towns even have three or four all in the same street. Surely Jesus didn't want his followers divided up into rival groups.'

Well, you're right. It is a waste. And unChristian. Churches *can* compete with each other. Jesus prayed that all his followers would be one. The Bible tells off some churches for being rivals. But there are also good reasons for different churches. Some get so far from the truth that people have to leave. The only way they can worship together is by forming a new church. Or different ideas develop about what is right, and splits occur.

The church has members from every nation on earth, too. Sometimes Christians from one place move to another. They might prefer to keep their own language and way of doing things. Would you want to worship God in a language and style that is foreign to you?

It's a matter of trying to balance love and truth.

Christians who go to war with each other, using their differences as the excuse, are wrong. Their belief in Jesus ought to be the thing that joins them together.

Jesus taught us to love one another, even our enemies. Yet, he also said a lot about truth. He didn't want people to be wishy-washy about following him. So Christians can't ignore what is just plain wrong, even in other Christians. But in each local church these issues don't come up very often. The main concern there is getting on with being Christians together.

How do you react?

1   *'It's nonsense. They're all hypocrites.'* (**turn to page 33**)
2   *'Makes some sense. I'd like to find out more about Mr Purdue's ideas on another matter.'* (**turn back to page 50**)
3   *'I'd like to get back to talking with the minister about Aunt Jane's funeral.'* (**turn to page 67**)
4   *'I'm tired from all this thinking. I'll head for the pub and a long relaxing drink.'* (**turn to page 74**)

This page is a guide to the questions in this book. It's more fun to read it as a story. But you might like to check here if there's anything else you want to ask.

Simply turn to that page and begin again. Or browse.

St Mark's Church, Aston
Minister: The Rev. William Purdue

St Mark's exists to help people know Jesus, and live their lives as his followers and friends.

We get together each Sunday to worship God, study the Bible, pray and share our concerns. You are welcome to join us.

There are some questions we're often asked. The books below give readable, reliable answers. You can buy them from the local Christian book shop or borrow them from the church library.

Does God exist? If so what is God like?
Understanding the Trinity, A. McGrath (Kingsway)

What does 'faith' mean and who is Jesus?
Finding Faith, A. Knowles (Lion)

What is Christianity all about?
Dead Sure? J. John (Frameworks)
Mere Christianity, C. S. Lewis (Fontana)
Real-life Christianity, A. Knowles (Lion)

What are Christians like?
Talking Heads, J. John and S. Cavill (Frameworks)

Don't forget the Bible! The *Good News Bible* is easiest to read. To get to grips with it, try
User's Guide to the Bible, C. J. H. Wright (Lion)

'Nice of a church to have something like that to give you,' you think. Then you say to yourself,

1 *'It's Saturday night. I'll go to the pub.'* (**turn to page 74**)
2 *'I couldn't get through another book now. But I'd like a start on knowing about Jesus.'* (**turn to page 39**)
3 *'Think I'm ready for the funeral now.'* (**turn to page 60**)

'All those stories of Jesus come from the Bible. Wasn't it all written years and years after things happened?' you ask. 'It might be all fairy stories, or at least, exaggerated. Can we even be sure Jesus existed?'

No serious historian doubts that someone called Jesus of Nazareth went around the land of Israel teaching and gathering followers. That eventually he became a problem for the authorities, so they had him killed. And that his followers claimed to have met with him, alive again. They began to worship him. That's history.

'But did the stories get distorted?' you wonder. 'They were all more religious in those days, weren't they?'

Well, for one thing, you shouldn't assume that people then would believe anything. They were used to people claiming to be God – and to being disappointed by them. Somehow, Jesus did not disappoint his followers, even after dying.

Also, Jesus' followers were all people who believed *strongly* in one God, who is in heaven. So what made them suddenly start talking about Jesus as God living with them on earth? Either they were very stupid, with insane ideas. Or they were pulling an enormous con job on the world. Or the Bible story about Jesus is true. Mad, or bad, or true?

'But weren't there years and years between the events and their being written down?' you think.

That doesn't mean the record is wrong. Take World War II for example. It's only now, 45 years or so later, that historians are starting to see its full significance. Lots of people who were in the war are still alive to check this work. But they may not be the best ones to explain the War because they were too close to it. There's less time between Jesus' life and when it was written down, than between World War II and us now!

(*If you asked about the Bible because you were thinking about Jesus,* **turn back to page 69.** *Otherwise,* **continue on page 80.**)

What do you think? Mad? Bad? Or true?
    'Jesus and his followers were (and are):

1 *'Mad. Christians are people with hang-ups.'* (**turn to page 25**)
2 *'Bad. Christianity can be dangerously deceptive. We live. We die. That's all.'* (**turn to page 32**)
3 *'True. I'd better find out more about God.'* (**turn to page 53**)

'Do Christians pray all the time? Do they really like going to church?' you ask yourself. 'Do they ever have any fun?'

Your aunt didn't seem to pray all the time. But she did pray quite often. She always said 'Thank you God' or something before meals at her place. 'It was so embarrassing that time when Dad and I got our food and started right in,' you remember. But Aunt Jane just smiled, and prayed, 'For what we are about to receive, and have already received, Lord make us truly thankful.'

When you and Pete camped in her garden, she said a prayer before she left you to the noises of the night. Made you feel safe. 'Say another one, Aunty,' pleaded Pete, not sure whether one short one would do. 'No,' she laughed, 'one is enough. God can be trusted to hear us. And I don't want to miss my film on the telly.'

Aunt Jane seemed to have time for ordinary fun as well as religion. In fact, she managed to make going to church seem like fun. She took you along once, and the church was full of her friends.

'It's dreadful how some people make church dull,' she'd say. 'Being a Christian means being interested in every part of life! I think our minister sets a very good example by following the football.'

Some churches, and some Christians, *are* boring. We admit it. But TV can get pretty boring, too. So can going to the pub, if none of your friends are there. So is the football, when your team's being thrashed!

What do you think?

1 *'The pub sounds a good idea.'* You head off there. (**turn to page 74**)

2 *'Why did Aunt Jane's God let her suffer, when she was such a good Christian?'* (**turn to page 63**)

3 *'I'd like to chat to the minister about my aunt.'* (**turn to page 67**)

4 *'Christians* do *go on about sin a lot.'* (**turn to page 64**)

Gambling hasn't appealed to you much before. But you feel a thrill as you think about pulling a jackpot.

Dad used to say it was a fool's game. 'Gamblers are like lonely drinkers. Losers. Headed for trouble.'

Aunt Jane agreed with him for once. She never gambled, but she didn't make a thing of it. 'You're right, Charlie. No-one truly appreciates anything they obtain by chance.'

She'd get annoyed, too, because Mum liked a flutter on the horses sometimes. 'Life didn't come about by chance,' she'd say. 'God doesn't want us to trust luck for food, fun, money, or anything else.'

Mind you, your aunt would nearly always buy a raffle ticket, 'If it helps a good cause.' You wonder what she'd do if ever she won!

What do you want to do now?

1 *Nothing. 'Life is just a matter of chance.'* (**turn to page 75**)
2 *Make a night of it, and drown your problems in beer.* (**turn to page 37**)
3 *Go home for a quiet Sunday before the funeral.* (**turn to page 60**)
4 *Think more about your aunt's ideas.* (**turn to page 14**)

The Lord's prayer jolts you back to reality. You find yourself repeating parts of it, imprinted on your mind from somewhere way back in your brain.

Our father . . . God – your father? You – God's child? You become more self-conscious, aware of your own voice.

All through the service you've tasted an amazing cocktail of emotions. You sense a tidal wave of grief about to overwhelm you. Yet so many people actually seem happy. Aunt Jane's life has given them so much to be thankful for. They seem so certain about where she is now.

Then Mr Purdue gets up to speak. His sermon is all about life after death, resurrection. It turns out that resurrection is not the same as simply coming back to life, like resuscitation given by an ambulance officer. It's to do with getting a new kind of body.

('Sounds like a lot more than just sorting out what you believe,' you think. 'More like a whole new way of life, complete with eternal, life-time guarantee!')

'Christians see life beyond death as a new start, with a new body, in a new world, where it all works how it is meant to work,' Mr Purdue continues. He makes each point by thumping his Bible.

'Jane showed us something of how that worked out in this world,' he says. ('That's a nice compliment,' you think.) He tells a few stories about her, and then prays again.

The service ends. Some men pick up the coffin. You realize that Dad is one of them. Mr Purdue leads them down the aisle.

You find yourself walking down the aisle behind Aunt Jane's coffin. Snatches of the service ring in your ears. 'Goodness and mercy.' 'Resurrection to eternal life.' 'Death, where is your victory?' 'In the midst of life we are in death.' And 'our father' again.

(*The story continues on page 84*.)

As you emerge from the church the sunlight dazzles you. People stand around for a bit, quieter now. A few shed tears. Mostly silence, broken by quick smiles. You won't forget the real joy which is there even in the sadness of the church members.

Only the family and a few close friends are going to the burial. No-one says anything on the way. You don't mind the silence. Words would spoil things now.

The coffin is put down next to a great big hole in the ground. All ready for Aunt Jane. You think it looks like a comfortable bed to rest in. Then it looks like a dungeon. You're feeling a bit mixed up.

You slowly make your way to stand near the mound of fresh earth. Mr Purdue carefully reads the words everyone has been waiting so long to hear.

> *We here commit the body of our sister Jane to the ground: earth to earth, ashes to ashes, dust to dust.*
>
> *In the name of our Lord Jesus Christ, who died, and was buried, and rose again for us.*
>
> *Thanks be to God who gives us the victory through Jesus Christ our Lord!*

The coffin is lowered into its home.

You pick up a clod of earth. It makes a dull thud when it hits the coffin. You walk away.

(*Please turn the page*)

Is that all there is?

Dead Sure?
about yourself, life, faith
J. JOHN

Team up a popular and experienced evangelist with a highly talented, full-colour illustrator and make the resulting book available at a truly affordable price. Then you have an effective and lively explanation of Christianity for today's young adult.

Dead Sure? combines an author who clearly understands his audience and a format that draws the reader in and 'speaks' alongside the text.

96 pages   *Large paperback*

FRAMEWORKS

How could God let this Happen?
Real lives in crisis
JIM LONG

Why does God let it happen? Suffering and pain are sensitively explored through actual, vivid testimonies of young people who have faced crisis. Each true case story is introduced, told and commented upon by the author, Jim Long, who himself suffers from a visual handicap. For him, each story illustrates a biblical landmark in a vital journey of discovery.

The stories describe terminal illness, a heart transplant, natural disaster, suicide, and violent attack, yet contain features that affect us all.

160 pages   *Pocketbook*

FRAMEWORKS

Talking Heads

J. JOHN and SUE CAVILL

Talking Heads is a series of eight profiles showing the relevance of Christianity to life in today's world. Simon Hughes MP and Roy Castle are included, as well as a former Sikh, a psychiatrist, a cerebral palsy victim, an ex-convict, a feminist and a company director.

Each answers common objections to faith in Christ and stimulates the reader to find out more. Powerful photographs and illustrations are used throughout. Here's a lively new book to give to those 'just looking' at Christianity, especially young adults.

96 pages　　　　*'B' format*

FRAMEWORKS